Baby Animals

Children's Nature Library

PUBLICATIONS INTERNATIONAL, LTD.

8 7 6 5 4 3 2 1

ISBN 0-88176-455-8

Written by Eileen Spinelli

Table of Contents

Introduction 4
Elephant 8
Polar Bear 10
Ostrich 12
Koala 14
Raccoon 16
Kangaroo 18
Swan 20
Zebra 22
Gorilla 24
Chimpanzee 26
Hippopotamus 28
Horse 30
Pelican 32
Lion 34
Stork 36
Giraffe 38
Sea Horse 40
Rabbit 42
Skunk 44
Sheep 46
Deer 48
Seal 50
Fox 52
Cow 54
Pig 56
Penguin 58
Dog 60
Cat 62

Introduction

Some baby animals are hatched from eggs; others are born live. Some baby animals are born in snug nests. Some are born under the water. Many animal babies are helpless when they are first born. Like human babies, they need their parents to give them food, warmth, protection, and love. In some animal families, both parents care for the babies. But in most animal families, mothers take care of the young.

Baby animals have a lot to learn. They must learn to hunt for food. They must learn to sense danger and protect themselves. Some babies need to learn to swim; others must learn to fly. Many baby animals are taught what they need to know by their parents. But play is another important way that baby animals learn about their worlds.

Introduction

Animal babies come in many shapes and sizes. A baby sea horse is so tiny you can barely see it. A newborn giraffe is tall enough to bump its head on the doorway of your room. Baby lions and tigers look like big kittens. Some baby birds seem to be all mouth with nothing but food on their minds.

In this book you'll meet many baby animals. You'll learn how they are born, who cares for them, and what they like to eat. Color photographs will show you the animal babies' homes, their mothers, and their favorite things to do.

Elephant

When a baby elephant is about to be born, its
mother invites one of her friends to come and
help. She keeps watch while the mother cleans
her newborn. About two days after it is born, a
baby elephant is able to travel with its mother.
But first it must learn to get along with its own
trunk. It always seems to be getting in the way.

Polar Bear

Baby polar bears are born in dens dug deep into the snow. The newborn cubs are so small that they can almost fit in your jacket pocket. When they are old enough, mother bear takes them out to explore. The cubs walk single file behind their mother. If they get tired, she pushes them along with her nose. Sometimes mother bear lets the cubs ride on her back.

Ostrich

An ostrich egg is the biggest egg there is. The eggshell is about as thick as a dinner plate.

Mother and father ostrich take turns sitting on their eggs. When it is time for an egg to hatch, the chick inside chirps. Some chicks peck out of their shells in a few hours; others take days.

When the chick is finally out of its shell, it is about one foot tall and very tired.

Koala

Baby koalas are very tiny when they are born.
They crawl across their mother's fur and snuggle
deep in her pouch. When baby gets too big for
the pouch, it climbs onto mother's back.
Sometimes, her baby is almost as big as she is.
Poor mother koala! If baby koala is naughty,
mother turns it over her knee and spanks it.
Poor baby koala!

Raccoon

When raccoon babies are first born, they just sleep and drink their mother's milk. But soon they are getting into everything. They poke into birds' nests. They chase after their brothers and sisters. They scamper up trees, only to discover that it's a lot easier to go up than it is to come back down. Mother raccoon is patient. But if her baby is naughty, she swats its tiny tail.

Kangaroo

A newborn kangaroo is so small it could easily sit on your finger. It is called a joey. As soon as joey is born, it crawls into its mother's cozy pouch.

There it drinks her milk and grows big and strong. If a mother kangaroo senses that she is in danger, she hides her joey in the bush. When she is sure it is safe, she comes back for her baby.

Swan

A baby swan is called a cygnet (SIG-nuht).
Cygnets look nothing like their beautiful parents.
They are gray and fuzzy, and look like big ugly
ducklings. But their mothers love them very
much. On a cold rainy day, mother swan shelters
her little ones under her wings. On bright sunny
days, she takes them for a spin around the lake
on her back.

Zebra

Baby zebra stands up a few minutes after it is born. Its legs are wobbly at first. But by the time it is one hour old, baby zebra can run. Young zebras like to chase their friends and play tag. Mother zebra pretends she is fighting with her baby. This game teaches it how to protect itself.

When baby is tired, it sleeps on the ground. Mother naps close by, standing up.

Gorilla

Gorilla babies begin to scamper about on all fours when they are six months old. Until then their mothers carry them.

During the heat of the day while mothers nap, baby gorillas tumble in the warm grass with their friends. They also like to play house and build their own little nests.

But at night when it's time to go to sleep, baby gorilla snuggles next to its mother in her nest.

Chimpanzee

When a chimpanzee is born, its entire family gathers to stroke and cuddle the new baby. When it is a tiny newborn, the baby chimp clings to its mother's belly. When it gets bigger, it rides on its mother's back. Brothers and sisters often babysit little chimps. If baby is grumpy or has a temper tantrum, the whole family ignores it for a while.

Hippopotamus

A baby hippopotamus
can swim before it
can walk. Like its
mother, baby spends
all day in the river.

When it wants to get somewhere in a hurry, a
baby hippo hitches a ride on its mother's back.

If she goes off to feed by herself, mother hippo
leaves her baby with one or two other female
hippos. You could say that baby goes to hippo
daycare.

Horse

A baby horse is called a foal. Very soon after it is born, a foal can stand up. In a few more hours, it is prancing around the meadow. A foal drinks milk from its mother, but it also nibbles grass. If the weather is bad and the horses are kept in their warm stalls, a foal will share its mother's dinner of oats.

Pelican

Mother pelican has a pouch attached to her lower jaw. She uses the pouch to catch fish, but she also uses it to feed her babies. Mother pelican chews up some fish, then she burps. A tasty meal of fish soup flows into her pouch. Her chicks drink the soup down to the last drop. You might say that a pelican's pouch is like a soup bowl.

Lion

When a lion cub is born, it is about the size of a house cat. Both parents look after the cubs. The lioness is a very good mother. She feeds her baby and licks it clean. Mother lion also plays with her cub. She lets it tug on her tail and climb up her legs. When the lion cub is three months old, it has its first hunting lesson. Soon it is ready to go out on its own.

Stork

Storks build their nests in treetops, church towers, chimneys, and other high places. Older storks are quiet, but baby storks never stop whistling and whining for food. Stork parents are kept busy flying to the edge of the nest with the chicks' next meal. When they are about two months old, it is time for the babies to begin flying lessons. Once the chicks begin to fly, they are called fledglings.

Giraffe

Mother giraffe is so tall that she gives birth standing up. Baby giraffe falls to the ground with a thump, but it doesn't get hurt. Maybe this first fall just gets the baby giraffe used to all the falls it takes while it is learning to stand up.

When it successfully gets up on all four feet about an hour after it is born, baby giraffe stands six feet tall.

Sea Horse

In almost all families, mothers give birth. But sea horses are different. Father sea horse gives birth to the babies. Mother places her brightly colored eggs in a pouch on father's belly. When the time comes for the little sea horses to be born, father gives his pouch a push with his tail. Out pop about 200 tiny babies. They have big eyes, and you can see through their skin.

Rabbit

Mother rabbit builds a snug nest with grass and soft puffs of her own fur for her babies.

When she leaves the nest and goes off to feed, the baby rabbits might get cold and catch the sniffles. To keep them warm, she covers the entrance to her nest with leaves and dirt.

A few weeks after they are born, baby rabbits begin to hop about and find their own food.

Skunk

When a baby skunk is first born, it is about the same size as a mouse and has very little hair. But two weeks later, its silky black-and-white coat has grown in. Baby skunks like adventure. They like to explore. Sometimes baby wanders too far from home. Then mother skunk goes after her baby and carries it home by the scruff of its neck.

Sheep

A baby sheep is a lamb.
Spring is the time when
most lambs are born.
A lamb usually has a
twin brother or sister.
It likes to stay very
close to its mother.

Even when a lamb grows up, it follows its mother
wherever she goes. Lambs and their mothers
know each other by their smells and by the way
they baa.

Deer

A baby deer stays
hidden in the woods
and waits for its
mother to feed it.

It lies so still that
you can't hear it.

It has no odor, so you can't smell it. You won't
know it is there unless you just happen to see it.
A baby deer is called a fawn. When it is two
weeks old, a fawn
is taken to meet its
father. The family
stays together until
winter. By then
the fawn is almost
full grown.

Seal

Most seal pups are born on land. But it isn't long until they are swimming in the cold sea next to their mothers. Baby seals play all the time. They splash and leap through the water. They blow bubbles and chase seaweed. They play tag with other pups. They seem to be having so much fun that soon the adults join in their game.

Fox

A mother fox is called a vixen. She has four, five, or six cubs at a time. Baby foxes are usually born in the spring. They are born with their eyes closed just like puppies. When the cubs are two weeks old, their eyes open. Soon their mother will take them out at night and teach them to hunt for food. Fox cubs will eat almost anything, but they like berries best.

Cow

A baby cow is
called a calf.

Soon after it is born,
a calf can stand up.
But it doesn't stay on
its feet very long.

A calf likes to rest on the cool grass near its
mother. If a calf wanders away from its mother,
it calls out to her, "I'm lost." Mother moos back
in a way that tells her baby that she is coming
to find it.

Pig

Just as soon as a pig is born, it wants to play. Baby pigs are called piglets. When they are newborn, they drink their mother's milk. Soon she takes them into the field. They watch her use her sturdy snout to root around in the earth for food. Then like little copycats, they root around too. Piglets are clean and smart. They are wonderful pets, but they get big quickly.

Penguin

Mother penguin lays a single egg. She passes the precious egg carefully to father penguin. He balances the egg on his feet. To keep it warm, he covers the egg with his belly. When the chick hatches, it is mother's turn to keep the baby warm. When the chick grows too big to snuggle under its parents, it huddles close to other young penguins to keep out the cold.

Dog

Puppies are born with their eyes and ears shut tight. By the time they are two weeks old, they can see and hear and the fun begins. Puppies play almost all the time. They run around the backyard. They chase their brothers and sisters. They chase anything that moves. They even chase their own tails. Puppies love to chew. If a puppy gets the chance, it will happily chew up your shoe.

Cat

Newborn kittens stay very close to their mother. Most of the time, they sleep or drink milk from their mother. When a kitten is a few weeks old, it begins to explore. Kittens are curious. They peek in closets and climb into open bureau drawers. They crawl under beds and play with dust balls and stray socks. Kittens like you to pet them if you are gentle.

Sheep and lamb